WORLD POLITICS
in 100 WORDS

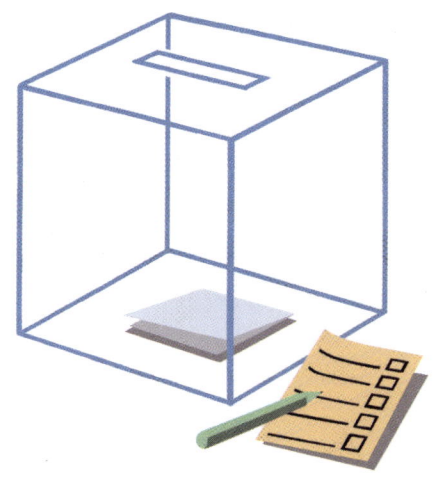

Quarto is the authority on a wide range of topics.

Quarto educates, entertains and enriches the lives of
our readers—enthusiasts and lovers of hands-on living.

www.quartoknows.com

Author: Eleanor Levenson
Illustrator: Paul Boston
Consultant: Emily Purser Brown
Designer: Victoria Kimonidou
Editor: Carly Madden
Creative Director: Malena Stojic
Publisher: Maxime Boucknooghe

First published in 2020 by words & pictures,
an imprint of The Quarto Group.
The Old Brewery, 6 Blundell Street,
London N7 9BH, United Kingdom.
T (0)20 7700 6700 F (0)20 7700 8066
www.quartoknows.com

A catalogue record for this book is available from the British Library.

ISBN 978 0 7112 5024 6

Manufactured in Malaysia TM042020

9 8 7 6 5 4 3 2 1

WORLD POLITICS
in 100 WORDS

Words by **ELEANOR LEVENSON**
Pictures by **PAUL BOSTON**

words & pictures

CONTENTS

State
Concepts that help explain how things are run and who makes rules about what can and can't be done.

Citizenship
Our role as individuals living in a society with other people.

Ideas
Thinking about the big and small things that affect the way we live our lives.

Look out for the symbols on each page. They show which theme the 100-word entry relates to. Some entries relate to more than one theme.

Politician

A politician is someone who tries to seek power so that they can have a say in how things are run. This could be at a local level, running a town, or a village, or at a national level running a whole country. Politicians create laws that the people living in that area have to follow, and decide how to run things according to the laws made by other politicians. For example, politicians running the country may decide to give money to a city for its schools, and the politicians in the city will decide how schools can use it.

Authority

Authority is the idea that the people in power have the right to be there. This might be because they have won an election, or because they have popular support, or in some countries it comes from the belief that they have been given authority by God or by other religious beings. Authority suggests that the people who are being told what to do accept that this is okay – a teacher, for example, only has authority over their class if the students accept that they should do what the teacher says. The 'authorities' refer to organisations with powers over people.

10   11

Economics

How to access the goods
and services we need
to live our lives.

Media

The way we give and receive
information about what is
going on in the world.

INTRODUCTION

Unless you live as a hermit, hiding out in an isolated cave and never seeing anyone or buying anything, then you need to understand politics. Whether you can go to school, whether you have healthcare when you are sick, what you can buy and sell, and even whether you are free to walk down the street when you want – all of these things are affected by the way politics work, the people who become politicians and the political decisions they make.

In every country the political systems and culture are different. But the first step to changing the world – or even to keeping it the same – is to understand how things work. This book tries to start that process for you, explaining some of the words and concepts that you will come across when you start to take an interest in politics.

And thinking about it, even hermits need to know this! Otherwise they won't know how to object if the politicians decide to take over all of the caves...

Politics

The Greek philosopher Aristotle wrote a book, *Politics*, in the fourth century BC, analysing the different ways of governing (being in charge) and the questions that arise from these. Not much has changed since. Today we use the word politics to refer to the people and processes involved in making decisions about how we live our lives, and how people try to achieve that power, such as running for election, making political friends (and enemies) who will help them on their path to power, and coming up with ideas for what they would do if they actually ever achieve this.

Democracy

In Greek, *demos* means 'people' and *kratos* means 'rule', so 'democracy' means
ruled by the people. Direct democracy means all citizens (people who are allowed to vote)
have a say on every issue, voting on each one. However, most democracies are representative
democracies, which means that citizens vote for representatives who then vote on legislation
on their behalf. Then these laws apply to all people equally. Democracy includes the acceptance
that the winners of elections, whichever system is used, are allowed to get on with governing.
People then accept the winners' decisions even if they did not vote for them.

Politician

A politician is someone who tries to seek power so that they can have a say in how things are run. This could be at a local level, running a town or a village, or at a national level running a whole country. Politicians create laws that the people living in that area have to follow, and decide how to run things according to the laws made by other politicians. For example, politicians running the country may decide to give money to a city for its schools, and the politicians in the city will decide how schools can use it.

Authority

Authority is the idea that the people in power have the right to be there.
This might be because they have won an election, or because they have popular
support, or in some countries it comes from the belief that they have been given authority
by God or by other religious beings. Authority suggests that the people who are being
told what to do accept that this is okay – a teacher, for example, only has authority
over their class if the students accept that they should do what the teacher says.
The 'authorities' refer to organisations with power over people.

Bureaucracy

Strictly speaking bureaucracy means the workforce of officials who run the administrative system of government or other large organisations, with bureaucrats being the people who work in them. The idea of the faceless bureaucrat refers to people working in administrative roles who follow rules and enforce regulations, with no personality or identifying features of their own to make them different to any of the other faceless bureaucrats. However, bureaucracy – or 'red tape' – has also come to be known as any paperwork or form filling that needs to be done in order to complete a task, often without an obvious reason.

Government

The word government is often used to mean those in charge, or running things, but government actually consists of three parts – a legislature, an executive and a judiciary. The legislature makes the law. The executive runs things according to the law. And the judiciary interprets the laws. Depending on how a country is organised, the same people may do more than one of these roles, or they may be completely separate (which is known as the separation of powers). The government represents the country in international matters and makes decisions such as whether to go to war or sign treaties.

Nation

Nation is the word for a group of people who see each other as being part of the same group, bound together by having something in common. This can be based on many things – having the same language, religion, history, traditions, culture or homeland. A nation does not have to have its own country, or geographical area, although it often does. If it doesn't then it is called a 'stateless nation'. The word nation is also often used to mean country, which is what is meant by the United Nations, the worldwide body representing all of the countries on Earth.

Sovereignty

The idea that a country is free to decide how it rules itself is called
sovereignty, so a sovereign state is one that governs itself. This means that whatever
form of government is in charge of making the rules in a country – whether it is an elected
government or an absolute monarch (a king or queen who decides everything) – it should
be able to do so without other countries and organisations interfering. In reality, countries are
bound by many treaties (agreements they sign with other countries) and by international
law, which are laws that govern the relationships between different countries.

Populism

Populism is when politicians claim their ideas represent ordinary people
while telling people that the existing politicians do not care about them. They look at
politics as a fight between ordinary people, who are the goodies trying to work hard to have
a nice life for their families, and people in charge, who are the baddies who don't care about
anyone other than themselves. Populists often blame particular groups for things that
have gone wrong, saying that the baddies are immigrants, or people with a particular
skin colour or religion, or those who are rich or have a good education.

Nationalism

Nationalism is the idea that the interests of a particular nation should be put before the interests of any other. This is usually tied in with a belief that this group of people should have their own sovereign country (country that rules itself) rather than being part of another country, which is why nationalism is a part of so many independence movements. Nationalism emphasises the differences between people, rather than the similarities, spreading the idea that each nation of people is distinct and placing focus on the importance of traditional languages, music, crafts and traditions, often in a populist way.

Anarchy

· ·

Anarchy is the idea of a society without government, laws or police. For some people the idea of such a society is horrifying and they fear it would lead to everyone treating each other badly without a sense of right and wrong. For others it represents a wonderful society, free from laws telling them what they can and can't do, in which people can organise themselves rather than needing governments to do it for them. If something is described as anarchy it usually means that there is chaos and confusion, and that no one is in charge or has control.

Legitimacy

Legitimacy means that something is recognised by most people as being the correct thing. A legitimate government is one that has gained power by winning fair elections, and laws are legitimate if they have been passed properly according to the rules of that country or organisation. So something is not legitimate in politics if it has happened by cheating or breaking the rules. Legitimacy means accepting the way a system works – you may not have voted for the person who wins an election, but you do accept the right of the person with the most votes to be the winner.

Policy

A policy is a set of beliefs or principles that is used to help make decisions. A political policy might, for example, be that all children should have access to free education. This policy would then guide legislation that makes this happen, such as laws ensuring there are schools in every area and that they are open to everyone. When a political party adopts a policy they are saying to voters that if they are elected they will work to make this happen. Policies are statements about what you will do when you are in a position to run things.

Platform

When a candidate or political party formally sets out what they would do if they were in power, in order to persuade voters to support them, it is called a platform – known as a manifesto when written down. They can help to show the differences between candidates when at first glance they might appear similar. Platforms are seen as promises to voters. Each promise is sometimes called a plank, the idea being that several planks of wood make up an actual platform to stand on, which political candidates would have done in the past when setting out their political platform.

Selection

To be chosen as the candidate to be on the ballot (the list of people you can vote for) on behalf of a political party, you first need to face selection. This is where you have the chance to persuade the party that you are the best person to be their candidate. This works differently in each country and in each political party but in every case the party must decide whether they want the person who would be best at the job or the person who would appeal to the most voters – sometimes this is even the same person.

Vote

· ·

When you say who it is you want to win an election, you are casting
a vote. There are many different ways to do this. Sometimes you go in
person to a polling station and write your vote on a piece of paper or put it
into a computer. Sometimes you vote by raising your hand in a meeting. In
some elections you vote directly for who you want to win. In others you
vote for a delegate who then casts their vote in a further election. In a
democracy every vote is worth as much as every other vote.

Empire

When a country rules over other countries, imposing laws and culture on its people, it is called an empire. Empires usually happen when the ruling country has taken over other places either by 'discovering' them and claiming the land as their own, or by winning a war to control that country. The Roman Empire, for example, was a huge ancient empire that grew larger as Roman forces invaded more land. Its capital was Rome and the Emperor (leader of the empire) was based there, and made all the laws, with less powerful leaders spread throughout the empire to enforce these.

Independence

When one nation is ruled by another, it may seek independence, which means it wants to become its own country with its own government making its own laws. In some cases this may mean leaving an empire. In others it may be leaving a union that was entered into willingly in the past. To be independent a country must define its borders and be recognised by other countries, usually by being admitted to the United Nations. The country may have to gain independence by winning a vote, by fighting a war, or through peaceful negotiation with the current governing country.

Executive

The executive part of a political system is the part of government with responsibility for running things and making important decisions. It is usually made up of the head of the government as well as the people appointed or elected to do particular jobs, such as being in charge of the departments responsible for things like defence, education, foreign relations and the economy. The executive decides how best to spend the money raised by taxes and provides some services to people such as education, a health service, the military and roads and infrastructure, although these are different in every country.

Legislature

The legislature is the part of government that makes the laws. In democracies the members of the legislature are elected, and laws (legislation) are voted on by members. Countries with bicameral legislatures have two 'chambers' or groups of people that legislation needs to pass through. The two chambers may be elected in different ways to each other, or one may be elected and one appointed or inherited. As well as voting on new laws, the legislature examines new laws to ensure they will work properly, and can sometimes make amendments (changes) to the law if they vote to do so.

Activist

What do we want? A definition of activism. When do we want it? Now!
For many people it is not enough to just think that something should change, they also want to do something to make this change happen. The people who do this are called activists. The things they do can be as varied as writing a letter, going on a protest or signing a petition. Or their activism may be less peaceful – some people try to disrupt day-to-day life for other people to make a point, or break the law in order for their cause to be noticed.

Grassroots

Ordinary people who make up the majority of those in an organisation or political party are considered to be the grassroots. As the name suggests, it means starting from the bottom (roots) up, so ideas that originate with ordinary members or activists, or leaders who emerge from this group of people, are considered to come from the grassroots. This is instead of ideas that start with leaders and then are communicated downwards to the rest of the organisation. If a politician is said to be losing touch with the grassroots it means they no longer know what ordinary people think.

15%

25%

35%

Poll

As with many words in politics, poll has more than one meaning.
Poll can be used to refer to an election, which is why some places call
the building where you go to vote a 'polling station' and talk about
'going to the polls'. But it can also be used to mean survey, so to take a poll
means you find out what a sample of people think about an issue. An opinion
poll will ask lots of people what they think and then apply the results
to the whole country in order to try to guess what will happen.

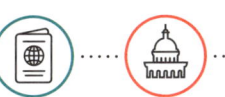

Referendum

Sometimes governments ask people to have a say on a particular issue by voting on it. In some countries it is the law that this must happen if the government wants to change the constitution. A plebiscite is the same thing as a referendum, although countries use each word slightly differently depending on the question being asked. Switzerland has more referenda (the plural of referendum) than any other country – they have several every year. Critics of referenda say that it takes power away from politicians, and allows populist arguments to persuade voters to do things without completely understanding the issues.

Education

Many people get their education in a school. Others might learn at home or teach themselves through practice or watching people. Education is when you learn things such as ideas, facts and skills. When politicians want to control people and take power away from them, they often stop them having access to education. Some countries don't let girls have an education; others only have education for people with enough money. Once you are taught something it is difficult to then un-know it, so education can change a person and the way they think about things, which some politicians find threatening.

Country

A country is a political and geographical term referring to an area of land,
usually with its own government and with national borders. This area is recognised by
other countries as having a right to exist. If you are a citizen of a specific country then,
unless it is occupied by another country, you will have that nationality (or have government
permission to live there – a visa). A country can make its own laws and apply them,
and is bound by international law, as well as being able to make its own
treaties with other countries and join international organisations.

Rights

Rights are the things you are allowed to do that are protected by the laws of where you live. However, not everybody approves of all of these rights. In some countries, for example, this might mean that you have the right to own a gun, and no one can stop you doing so. These are legal rights. Human rights are the rules that most people and countries think every person should have, such as the right to love who you want, the right to a family and the right to education, although not everyone agrees on what these rights are.

Responsibility

Responsibility means it is up to you to take charge of something.
In politics this is usually used to mean there are certain things you have to do
to play a full role in your country, and in return for the things the government
does. So politicians might promise to keep you safe and healthy by providing good
laws, police officers and a health service, and in return your responsibility may
be to stay as healthy as you can, not waste resources and not break the law.
It's about being a sensible person who works for the good of everyone.

Utopia

Thomas More, a sixteenth century English philosopher, first used the word utopia for his book about a made up island of the same name. Life on the island of Utopia was perfect. People who criticise this idea say such a place is not possible because not everyone wants the same thing, so some people will always be unhappy. Therefore utopia is usually used to mean that someone is imagining a perfect life that is not possible. If someone says you are imagining a utopia, they probably mean you are daydreaming or imagining things will be better than they can be.

Dystopia

The opposite of utopia is dystopia. A dystopia is an imagined society where people suffer unfairly, often the result of corrupt or controlling governments. This includes people not being able to get things they need like food, or businesses controlling every part of life, and people not being able to make choices about who they love and the work they do. In books and films this often happens after the world has suffered a disaster and a new society has sprung from the ruins. If someone calls something a dystopia they mean society is not working and people are suffering.

Feminism

Wanting women and girls to be treated equally to men and boys in terms of choices and opportunities is called feminism. Sometimes the issues are obvious, such as when women have less education than men or do not have their own money, but it also includes things like not being able to participate in sport, being expected to look a certain way, having to do all the housework or there being fewer women in certain jobs. Feminists usually believe that society has been set up to favour men, because the economic and political roles have been largely held by men.

Tolerance

In a free society people are able to live their lives the way they want, as long as they do not harm others. This means they can love whoever they want, whether it be a man or a woman, choose their own religious beliefs and hold any opinion that they wish. Tolerance is when you accept that people have a right to do this, whether or not you agree with their choices or viewpoints, and live happily side by side without restricting each other's right to do so. To be tolerant means you, individually and as a country, welcome diversity.

Propaganda

Propaganda is the word used for messages put out by a particular cause or political party, in order to influence how people think and act, often by choosing the facts to support their argument rather than by presenting a balanced view. This can be using any form of media – so propaganda can be a poster, a leaflet, a work of art, a film, a tv show or even a message on social media. A poster showing only the good things about a politician, or an image showing how life was good during a particular time, are both examples of propaganda.

Spin

There is really nothing bad about spin – it just means that political messages have been made easy for the public to understand. If you believe this, then you have just fallen for some spin about spin! In reality, spin means presenting a version of the facts to give a particular view of events instead of the whole truth. Spin, for example, might tell you that a particular policy is good for people, without mentioning all of the bad bits. The experts who help to create spin, which is a form of public relations, are often referred to as spin doctors.

Media

The media refers to the ways that people can be communicated to in big groups. Newspapers, television, radio and the internet are forms of media, and the word is often used to mean the people working to produce these, such as journalists and programme makers. Politicians need the media to get their messages to the people, but the media's job is to search for the truth and to communicate this to the people. When the media is owned by the state it means it is controlled by the government, which means it can't be trusted to look for the truth.

Pundit

A pundit, sometimes called a 'talking head', is an expert who gives easy to understand observations and analysis (saying what is happening and why) to the media to help people understand the issues in the news. They might explain what is happening and give background and context on the subject, or make predictions about what will happen next. Because they speak with authority – sounding like they are definitely correct – people will take what they say seriously. However, some pundits are willing to give an opinion on anything, whether they know much about the subject they are talking about or not.

Poverty

Poverty is when you don't have enough money to buy the basic things you need in life such as food, housing, clothes, healthcare and education. You can be considered to be living in poverty if you have much less than other people in your society – this is called relative poverty and may not be immediately obvious, as someone may have enough to eat and a home to live in but compared to other people in the same country they may have much less. Politicians can be judged on how many people live in poverty, and how they are looked after.

Wealth

Two people may have the same amount of money but one may live in a country where this can buy a lot and one may live in a country where it can buy little, so only the first person has wealth. Therefore how much money you have – or how many things that could be exchanged for money – can only really be understood when you look at how much things cost. When countries are wealthy it means the people have a high standard of living – lovely houses to live in, enough to eat and lots of luxuries (things they don't need).

Capitalism

If you give money to a food shop when you buy food, or a clothes shop when
you buy clothes, or any other shop to buy anything else, and some of that money ends
up in the bank account of the person who owns the shop, then you live in a capitalist
system. Capitalism is a system where trade – buying and selling – is done by businesses
rather than the government, with the aim of making money (profit) for individuals.
In theory, competition for custom leads to innovation and progress, although
critics say it leads to cost cutting and safety concerns

Socialism

Socialism is a political ideology that believes we will get a fairer society if the means of production are managed by the state or by the workers, rather than by private owners. Means of production are the materials used to make things, the tools and machinery with which things are made, and the factories and other places where they are made. Some modern forms of socialism believe in keeping a market economy (buying and selling things for profit) but with rules from government to make wealth more equal, although for many socialists this is a 'sell-out' and not real socialism.

Economics

. . . .

All of the things we use and make, including our own time and skills, are
called resources. The study of these resources is called economics. This can be split
into macroeconomics and microeconomics. Macro means big, such as looking at how much
money a country has or what a country produces. Micro means small and means looking
at how individuals, families and businesses make, buy and use the things that cost money.
Economists study this and then guess what will happen in the future based on their
research and their understanding of human behaviour, so that they can plan ahead.

Treasury

The part of government in charge of the money is sometimes called the Treasury, though it is often called other things such as the Ministry of Finance or Finance Department. It is the department that takes the money raised from taxation and decides how much money the government can spend on running things (a budget). This means that the head of the Treasury is usually very powerful because other departments need the Treasury to give them money to run all the things they are meant to run.

It can also mean a place where the money – the treasure! – is kept.

Budget

If you make a list of all the money you expect to have to spend and all the things you intend to spend it on, this is a budget. In political terms, a budget is exactly the same thing, although the money comes mainly from tax and from bonds (a way people and businesses can lend the government money) and the spending is mainly on services such as health, education, defence and infrastructure (buildings, roads, etc). So a budget is the government's way of telling you how much money they have and what they are going to spend it on.

Debt

Debt, in national terms, is when a country owes money that the government
has borrowed. This can be from ordinary people who have bought government bonds –
a way of saving where you lend the government money – or from other countries or
international organisations. Debt can help the government to invest in helpful things
for the country, just as a family might take on a debt for a new car or a better home.
But if a country has too much debt, then it will need to spend less on public
services (known as austerity) in order to pay it back.

Left

Politicians and ideas are often described as being on the left or the right,
also called left-wing and right-wing. This began during the French Revolution when
those sitting on the right of the King supported the monarchy as it was and those sitting
on the left supported reform. People on the left usually support the state being involved with
people's lives, controlling the economy and public services. The left believes in redistribution,
using tax as a way to address inequality by taking money from the rich to use on
services that everybody can use, and welfare systems for poorer people.

Right

. . . .

Economically, people on the right usually want how much things cost to
sort itself out using supply and demand (how much is available and how many
people want it), rather than the state imposing rules about what can be bought and sold.
The right tends to be relaxed about wealth inequality and that some people are very rich
while others have very little. Right-wing people tend to place lots of emphasis on individual
responsibility, and on looking after your own family unit. People can be socially
on the left but economically on the right, and also the other way round.

War

When people have a disagreement and try to solve the argument by seeing which is the strongest, it is called a fight. When the fight is between countries, and uses violence, it is called war. Sometimes wars begin by one country wanting to claim land from another country. At other times, a government may dislike something being carried out by the government of another country and see it as their job to stop it. Civil war is when groups within a country fight each other. International humanitarian law sets out rules for war, such as how to protect medical workers.

Treaty

When two or more countries make a formal agreement it is called a treaty. The treaty becomes part of international law and the countries have to stick to what they agreed. Treaties are about things like how to trade with each other, where the borders of a country are, ending a war, or taking action on an issue such as environmental damage. A treaty is more than a promise because once it has become international law, then the country has to stick to it whether they like it or not, unless the original agreement included ways to leave the treaty.

Leader

A leader is the person officially in charge of an organisation. A country's leader is usually the head of the government. Political parties have leaders too, as do most organisations. For example, a protest group will have a person or people who decide what to do and how and when to do it. The leader does not always have the power, though. They may have to do what their members tell them to or have powerful individuals running things behind the scenes – but they act as a figurehead, the person who represents the group to people in the wider world.

Dictator

A dictator is a leader who has a large amount of personal power, making all
of the rules and decisions alone. They usually abuse this power and do whatever
it takes to stay as dictator, such as using secret police to spy on their own people
and making laws that are good for their supporters rather than for everybody in society.
Dictators often stop people from being allowed to criticise them, and try to look
even more important by having statues and posters of their image everywhere.
A dictator that does not do bad things is called a benign dictator.

Corruption

··

The English politician and historian Lord Acton said, "Power tends to corrupt, and absolute power corrupts absolutely," meaning it is very hard to be in politics and not be corrupt on some level. Corruption is when people in positions of power act dishonestly for their own good rather than the good of everybody. This can be on a personal level, such as taking money to do something, like give information to someone who shouldn't have it or vote in a particular way, or on an institutional level, such as giving government work to friends in return for support or favours.

Scandal

A scandal is anything that shocks ordinary people. In politics this can be a politician being caught breaking the law or doing something naughty, such as having more than one boyfriend or girlfriend at the same time, or doing something because they have been given money rather than because it is the right thing to do, or giving a job to a friend rather than the best person for the role. The media likes scandals because, as well as ensuring politicians are acting correctly, it makes people want to read their articles, so journalists will often try to uncover them.

Petition

In ancient Egypt, slaves, cross about their working conditions, sent documents to their rulers asking for improvements. Historians now think this was the first example of a petition. If lots of people put their name to a request to do something it is called a petition. These can range from the simple – a sheet of paper on which someone asks you to write your name – to formal documents or websites that go straight to people in charge. They are used as a peaceful way of showing those in power how many people feel strongly about the subject of the petition.

FREE EDUCATION FOR ALL

END POVERTY

LISTEN

SAVE THE WORLD

CHANGE NOW

EQUAL RIGHTS

Protest

When you actually do something to show that you don't like the way things are, instead of just thinking that you don't like it, that is a protest. This can be small acts like refusing to stand up when someone important walks into the room or clapping your hands slowly during a speech, or a big act such as marching side by side with millions of other people in a demonstration. Sometimes small acts are actually big acts in terms of impact, such as Rosa Parks refusing to move from her seat on the bus during racial segregation in America.

Allies

When countries or people work together to achieve a common goal, they are said to be allies, or in an alliance. A political alliance is when political parties formally agree to work together, either contesting an election as one group or forming a coalition government (a government made up of more than one party) after an election. Allied forces, or allied powers, is the name given to specific group of countries working together in war, who share weapons and information against a common enemy. The countries that fought together against Germany in World War II are known as the Allies.

Republic

Over half of the world's countries use the word 'republic' (from the Latin *res publica*) in their title. The word, which means 'public affair', acknowledges the country belongs to the people, not to the rulers, and the Head of State (person who represents the country to other countries) does not inherit the role the way a king or queen does. Not all countries that use the word republic in their name are really democracies, but the word suggests that there are elections and a constitution, and that one person or group of people does not have all of the power.

Candidate

In ancient Rome people who put themselves forward for a political role would
wear bright white togas so that they stood out in a crowd. This led to the word candidate
which comes from the Latin word *candidus* – meaning 'bright white'. Nowadays, candidates
often try to look as much like the people they want to represent as possible, rather than
stand out. The word covers everyone seeking election, whether as a representative
of a political party or not, although once they have been selected by a political
party to stand under their banner, they are also often called a nominee.

Constituency

Constituency is the word given to the group of people who are represented by someone who has been elected, and also to the geographical area that the person represents (although some elections are based on things other than geography). The geographical area can also be called many other things such as election district, ward, precinct or division. Although not everyone in a constituency will have voted for the person or people who won the election, the job of the winner is to represent everyone who could have voted (and also those in that area who cannot vote, such as children).

Debate

A debate is the formal discussion of a subject in which people give opposing views and explain why they think what it is they think. A debate between politicians often ends in a vote – in democracies the government needs to win votes like these in order to create new law. Public debates are where politicians argue against each other in order to win public support. In the days and weeks before an election people trying to be elected might have one or more debates in person or on television, where they say what they would do if they were elected.

Rhetoric

The art of speaking persuasively is called rhetoric. Politicians making a speech need to be good at doing this in order to make people believe in their vision of what they want to do. There are lots of recognised rhetorical techniques that can be used to get attention and be memorable. Repetition is a good example of this. (I said, repetition is a good example of this!) So is hyperbole, which is making an exaggerated statement, and alliteration (using words beginning with the same letter). This book, for example, is the best book you will buy in a billion years.

Party

When people share a set of political beliefs they might get together and form a political party. Each party usually has its own set of rules about how they will choose their leader, select their candidates and decide which policies they would put in place if they were in charge. Members of a political party usually agree on general principles such as how the economy should be run or how a country should be organised, although they may disagree on the detail. Some countries only have one party, and the competition for power is between different groupings within that party.

Opposition

The opposition is the name for political parties who have some elected political representatives but are not the party of government. Healthy democracies have strong oppositions whose job is to challenge and scrutinise the government in order to ensure the legislation they introduce is justified and works. Oppressive states may try to repress the opposition and stop them doing their job, making the lives of people in the opposition difficult or making the existence of the opposition illegal. Some oppressive regimes deliberately create small opposition parties to make it look like they are a democracy even when they are not.

Committee

The groups of people who make decisions are often too large to be able to have proper discussion about issues. A committee is a smaller group of people who look at things in detail in order to accomplish a specific task. The tasks may include ensuring a piece of law is well written or making suggestions about how things can be done. The committee then makes recommendations to the people in charge. The person who runs the committee and is responsible for deciding what things are discussed and who can speak, is called the Chair (sometimes Chairman, Chairwoman or Chairperson).

Scrutiny

The word scrutiny means to closely examine something. In politics this usually means politicians examining the work of other politicians to ensure things are being done in the best possible way, without making laws that are unclear or spending money that isn't needed. They do this by asking official questions of politicians and experts and going through legislation (new laws) in detail in meetings often called committees. Media scrutiny means journalists observe what is happening closely, and public scrutiny means that the people are doing this – essentially it means being watched closely to make sure nothing bad is going on.

Citizen

....

Officially the word citizen means that you are a 'member' of a particular country, and that you have whatever rights other people there have, such as the right to vote or to own land. However, the word citizen has started to be used for more than this — to suggest anything that is done by an ordinary person (rather than someone employed to do a particular job). A citizen's arrest for example is when an ordinary person, rather than a police officer, arrests someone, and citizen journalism is when someone reports on a story rather than leaving it to a journalist.

Class

The political philosopher Karl Marx said class (also known as social class) is about whether you make money by working for other people or having people work for you. But people can be viewed differently for many reasons, such as being born into a particular type of family, the job they do, the property they own, how much education they have or the way they speak and the clothes they wear. Together these make you a certain class, which can affect the way you live and your ambitions, as well as how others view you and how you view yourself.

Constitution

A set of principles or fundamental beliefs that govern how an organisation or state should act is called a constitution. If it is written down in a document or set of documents, it is known as a written constitution. If a constitution is made up of many laws, precedents (previous decisions made by judges interpreting the law) and conventions (unwritten practices that have always been followed) but not written down in one place, it is an unwritten, or uncodified, constitution. Constitutions also say what it is that governments and rulers can and cannot do, and guarantee the rights of citizens.

Equality

In many places around the world people are treated unequally because of
who they are, for example women, gay people, those born into certain religions or with
certain skin colours or those belonging to different social classes. Equality doesn't mean
that everybody is the same, but that everybody is treated fairly despite their differences.
Equality means that people have the same rights and opportunities, so that in a democracy
everybody's vote is worth exactly the same; everyone is treated the same way if they
break the law and has access to the legal system if they feel something is unjust.

Globalization

When you buy something from another country or communicate with someone on the other side of the world, you are part of what is known as globalization, which means people, governments and businesses around the world can communicate, trade and share information. Some people see this as a bad thing because they think richer societies will take over and impose their way of life on poorer countries, exploiting their resources and destroying their traditions and way of life. But others embrace the idea as it allows for the exchange of ideas, information and skills, and to learn about other cultures.

Ideology

The main idea behind a set of policies is called an ideology. When you
have an ideology, the things you believe in, and the changes you want to make to
everyday life, are in order to get closer to a society that carries out your ideology.
For example, if your ideology is socialism you believe things that benefit society as
a group are more important than individual freedom, whereas if your ideology is
liberalism it is the opposite of this, and you believe that individual freedom
is far more important than the wants and needs of society as a whole.

Industrialization

When a country or society changes from being one that is mainly based on farming to one based on making things with machines and in factories, it is called industrialization. This usually happens after something monumental has been invented, like a new type of engine or a new way to create electricity. As more jobs become available in factories and there are fewer jobs on farms, people move to cities to look for work. Then the whole way people live, from what they eat to how they spend their time and who lives in their house, changes. This is industrialization.

Unions

If people who work in similar types of jobs join an organisation to protect their rights in the workplace, it is called a trade union. Unions work on the idea that people are stronger when they join together to ask for more money or better conditions – this is called collective bargaining. They also help members who have problems in the workplace, such as losing their job, and provide services such as education and social groups. If they don't get what they want, they can organise all of their members to stop working. This is called industrial action or a strike.

GDP

· ·

If you add up the value of all the things a society makes and all of the
services it provides, you get the Gross Domestic Product (GDP). Economists
and politicians care about this because if the GDP is increasing, it means the country
and its people are getting richer. Ordinary people are less concerned with this as they
know that things don't need to cost money to be important – falling in love, for example,
or caring for someone. But the GDP does allow politicians to compare how well
they are doing economically with other countries, and with its own record.

Trade

Trade is the buying and selling of things – this can be actual things like cars, computers or chocolate, or services such as teaching, care and information. Usually trade involves giving money to the person or organisation you are buying from in a system known as a market. A free market has no rules about prices and what can and can't be sold. If you swap one thing for another, such as a horse for magic beans – then this is known as bartering. Countries have agreements with each other over what they can trade and how much tax they can charge.

Property
··

If you own something you have property – this could be something big,
like land, or small, like a book or ornament. If something is your property you
have the right to use it, sell it, give it away or even destroy it (as long as doing
any of this does not break the law). Public property is owned by the country and
looked after for the people by the government. In the past, in many countries
you had to own land in order to be allowed to vote, and you were
seen as being more important than people without property.

Tax

··

When governments make you give them money, this is called tax.
Sometimes this is taken directly from the money that you earn, sometimes you pay
it as extra when you buy something, and sometimes you are made to pay it based on
where you live or the value of your home. These taxes are then used by the government
to provide the things that everyone needs such as schools, hospitals and roads. In
some countries, rich people have to pay more tax than poorer people. In others,
everyone pays the same rate. This kind of decision is made by politicians.

Patriotism

Originally the word patriot meant from a particular country or 'homeland', so a compatriot was someone from the same place. These days patriotism is used to describe an intense feeling of love and loyalty to your own country. This often includes love for the actual land, and feeling that only a specific place can be home. Because patriots love their country above all others, it can cause divisions and mean that those who criticise a country or have loyalties to more than one country get called unpatriotic, which can lead to people being made to feel unwelcome or treated differently.

Racism

The belief that some people are better than others based on the colour of their skin or their ethnicity is called racism. Throughout history some countries have been racist, treating groups of people differently either using official laws or by encouraging people to act in a racist way. A tolerant and democratic society will have laws to ensure that people cannot act on any racist beliefs they hold – so that they cannot stop people having a job, a home or access to services (like education and healthcare) based on this, and cannot urge others to act in a racist way.

Federalism

Federalism is a system where power is divided between different types of government, with one central government covering the entire country and smaller federal governments covering specific geographical areas. Each of these has its own clearly defined powers and each is of equal status (neither more important than the other). In this system the central government (the one that makes decisions for the whole country) can't tell the federal governments what to do, unlike non-federal systems where the central government still has control over local governments. Examples of federal countries are Germany, Brazil, India, South Africa and the United States.

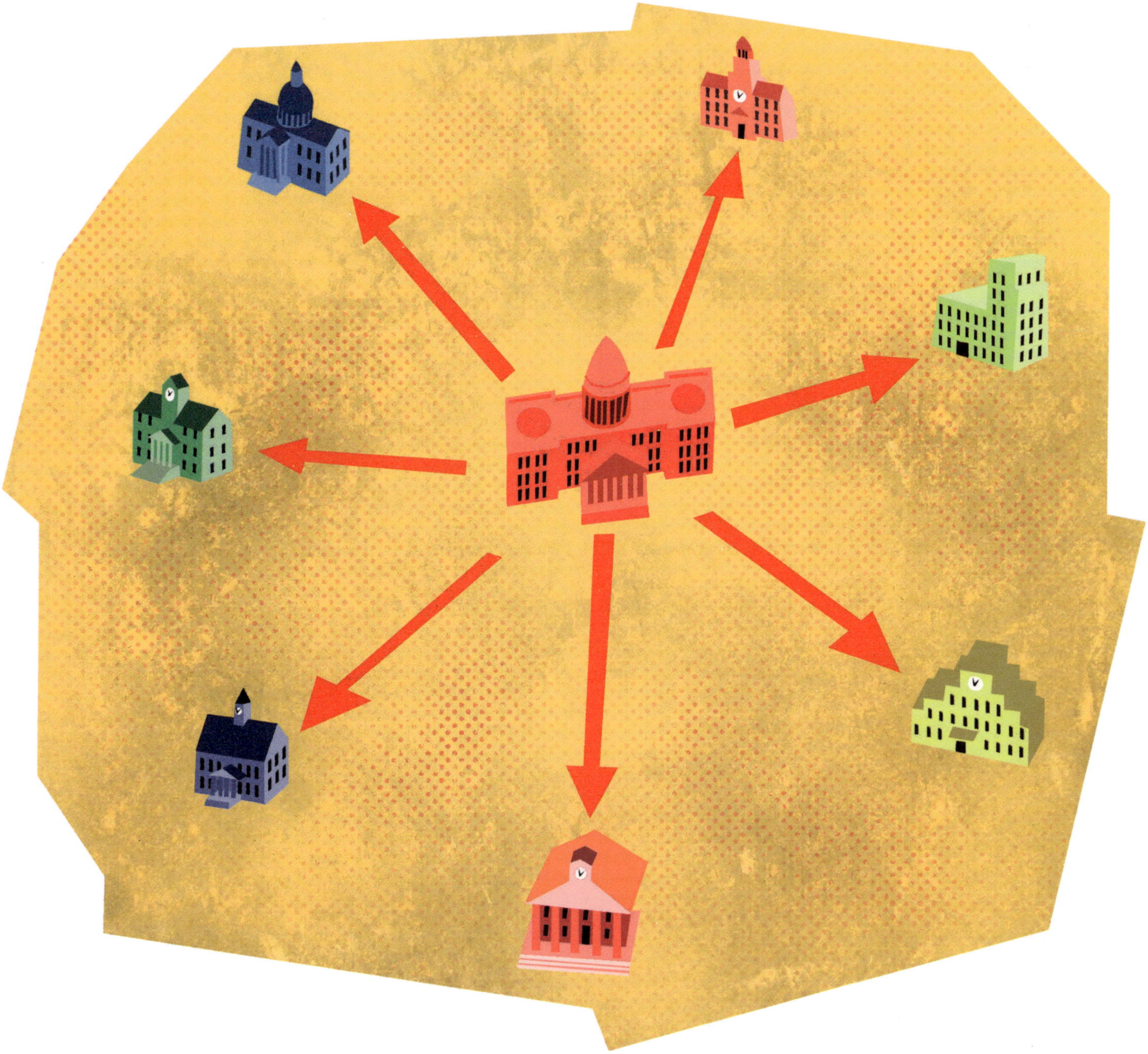

Localism

When the main government of a country passes power down to governments of smaller geographical areas – and these can be known by different names depending on each country – this is called localism, or devolution. Each level may have certain powers and obligations to make laws, raise taxes and provide services. In turn these may also have smaller governments under them serving smaller communities. The idea is that smaller – local – governments can better respond to the specific needs and ideas of the people they serve. If a country is very large even their local governments may look after millions of people.

Religion

Religion is a set of beliefs that combines living according to a set of rules with faith, or belief, that these rules are the right way to do things. Most, but not all, religions include a belief in a god or gods, and seek to explain how the Earth was made and what happens when people die. It is important in politics because some countries demand that their leaders are religious, and some specifically keep religion completely separate from politics. In religious countries this can sometimes be used to judge whether the politician has the right character for the job.

Secularism

If you do not live a religious life or identify as a particular religion, you are secular. In politics it means that religious organisations are completely separate to political ones, so that religious leaders do not get a political job without being elected, that religious laws do not form part of the country's laws, that schools funded by the government are not associated with a religion, and that political decisions are not influenced by religion. In a secular state people are free to choose which religion they follow and are also free to choose no religion at all, without repercussions.

Communism

Under communism, individuals cannot own property or make a profit, and any wealth that is created belongs to the state. This wealth is then, in theory, distributed equally according to need, although in practice the rulers usually get more. Politically, communist countries are often one party states (with no opposition parties) and no one is allowed to dissent (disagree with the government). Attempts to create communist societies have been characterised by oppressive dictatorships that have killed millions of people. It is not always simple, however – China is an example of a country that is politically communist but also economically capitalist.

Revolution

When the way society is organised changes completely, and quickly, it is called a revolution. A revolution can, for example, turn a society from capitalist to communist, or from a dictatorship to a democracy. Revolutions happen when enough people get together to demand change, and start with what one writer described as, "a spark electrifying the grumbling discontent of a million people." The word can also describe a complete change in the way we live or work. The Industrial Revolution happened when things began to be mainly made in factories and many people moved to cities to work in them.

Personality

Your personality is what makes you different to everyone else. You might be cheeky or kind or thoughtful or mean, or all of these at different times and in different amounts. In politics the personality of the leader has an impact on the way the country views itself and is viewed by others. If a leader is racist, for example, it will make it seem acceptable for ordinary people to be racist too. A 'cult of personality' is when leaders use propaganda to present an image of themselves as perfect, with special qualities that suggest they were destined to lead.

Endorsement

A political endorsement is when an individual or group makes a public declaration of support for a candidate or political party. This may or may not be helpful for the person being endorsed. If an organisation that supports people owning guns endorses a candidate, for example, it might put off people who don't approve of guns from voting for that person. Sometimes people want to look like they are powerful or successful by association, or to be in favour with whoever is in charge, so they will give their endorsement to the person they think is most likely to win.

Monarchy

A monarchy is a country where a king or queen (sometimes another title is used)
is the Head of State, which means they are the person who represents the country.
In absolute monarchies this person is also in charge of making laws. In places where there
are also elected politicians who make laws, the king or queen's role is mostly ceremonial
(going to events on the government's behalf). This is called a constitutional monarchy.
In a monarchy the job of monarch – the top representative – is usually hereditary,
which means it passes down to their oldest child when the monarch dies.

Military

Military is the word used for the organisations of people whose job it is to defend a country, although some countries use their military to attack other countries or even their own people. The organisations that make up the military can include the army, which is land-based, the navy, which works on the sea, and the air force, which operates from the air, as well as secret groups that carry out missions governments don't want people to know about. The military usually wear uniforms and follow strict rules. If the military turns against its own government, the government may fail.

Election

There are many ways of choosing who gets a job as a political representative.
Sometimes people inherit a role; some are picked randomly from people who put their
names forward; others are drawn from eligible candidates. The most common way in modern
history, however, is by having an election, which is when people vote for the person or party
they most want to win. It is a way of groups making decisions when various people
within the group want different things. Voting systems vary – sometimes you vote
for more than one candidate at once or give more than one choice.

State

However good you think you would be at it, you can't just set up your own
private police force, demand taxes, start an army or open a prison and send people
there. Only the state can do this. State is different to government – the government
sets policy and takes on responsibility for running the state, but the state is the system
and set of organisations that they are running. The state also runs services – these are
different in each country but can include schools, healthcare and any other
part of the system that is run by any form of government.

Lobby

When any organisation or individual tries to influence politicians to do something, it is called lobbying. Lobbying companies do this on behalf of their clients who pay them to help access decision makers and get their message across. Critics of this say that politicians should be acting in the national interest (whatever is best for the country) and not be influenced by whoever has been the most persuasive. Lobbyists aren't allowed to pay politicians to make decisions – that would be bribery – but the bigger their budget the more they can spend on events, stunts and materials to communicate their message.

Environmentalism

Environmentalism is the name for the kind of political beliefs that prioritise concern for the environment and the impact humans have on it. These are issues such as climate change, pollution, waste disposal, deforestation, water scarcity and wildlife conservation. It seeks to minimise the impact of humans on the planet, and fights to preserve the existing climate, resources and types of animals that exist on the Earth. The colour green is most commonly associated with environmentalism as it gives a sense of plants, nature and the regrowth associated with spring, and therefore environmentalist political parties are often known as 'Greens'.

Law

Rules that are made by the government, rather than, for example, by
your parents or your school, form the law. At the heart of this idea is justice,
which is about ensuring that life is fair and that the law is applied to all. By living in
a country, you are bound by its laws, and also by the power of the country's courts.
In court, punishment can be given out or justice applied according to the law.
Countries make laws in different ways. Dictators may just decide them, but
democracies make laws by having their politicians vote on them.

Judiciary

To work effectively countries need laws and these laws need people who can rule on what should happen when there are disagreements. The judiciary does this, listening to arguments in court and then deciding, either alone or in a group, what the law means. Judges also apply the law when people are in dispute with one another over rights or property, and decide whether someone is guilty or innocent in criminal cases and what their punishment should be. Many countries also have a jury system where a panel of ordinary people make the decision whether someone is guilty or not.

Liberal

Liberalism is an ideology that emphasises the importance of individual freedom. Liberals want people to be able to live their lives however they wish, as long as they are not hurting others, and to be able to trade freely. As well as individual freedoms (rather than being told what to do by the state or religious bodies), liberals usually believe in equality (everybody having the same rights) and representative democracy (everybody's vote being equal). Liberalism developed as a reaction to people having few freedoms, when monarchs had power to make rules without consultation, and people inherited their position in society.

Conservative

If you are a conservative then you probably do not like things to change in a big way. Conservative means you have traditional values, including the importance of the family unit, and that you want any changes to society to happen slowly, taking a cautious approach in order to see how things develop. Conservatives believe in individual responsibility rather than the state controlling people's lives, and that people should be able to own their own property and buy and sell things in a free market without too much interference from the government and without having to pay lots of tax.

Values

Values are the core beliefs that people have. That is, the sense of what is right and wrong, which in turn makes them believe in specific policies and ways of doing things. A politician might talk about their values as a way of showing the kind of person they are and to give a hint at where they are on the political spectrum (whether they are more left-wing or right-wing). Political parties will have shared values – things that ideally all its members and representatives believe in, and a country may even have values that they believe define the national character.

Coup

If you want to seize control of a country and kick out the current government, without going through the hassle of winning an election, then you need to stage a coup (short for *coup d'état*). To do this you will first need to get the support of the military and police. Be careful, though – if you stage a failed coup you are likely to be dealt with harshly and imprisoned for life, or killed. A democratic coup gets rid of an undemocratic government using force but then goes on to hold elections so the people can elect a democratic government.

Liberty

If you are free to make your own choices about how you live your life – as
long as you do not hurt others – without the government making laws that stop this
for no good reason, then you have liberty. For many countries, such as France – where
the nation's slogan is Liberty, Equality, Fraternity – the concept of liberty is an essential
part of their national identity (what it means to belong to that country). Liberty also
means freedom – so prisoners do not have their liberty, and slaves, who have
no choice but to work without any payment, are also not free.

Happiness

Happiness has become an important political word in recent years as economists and politicians in countries across the world have started to discuss judging the success of a country by how happy its people are rather than by how wealthy the country is (GDP). This includes things like the quality of the environment and whether people are healthy. In one country, Bhutan, they even have happiness as a goal of their constitution, and measure the Gross National Happiness (GNH), although this has been criticised by some as covering up the poverty and human rights issues that can be found there.

AUTHOR'S NOTE

It's a real challenge to define 100 political concepts, let alone to do so in 100 words, but I think it's really important to demystify politics and to make it a subject that everybody can understand, whatever their age. Once we start to understand how things work, we can start to work out how much we want to be involved in politics, whether it is casting our vote every few years and then forgetting about it, or working to change laws and systems. Every political journey is different but they should all have one thing in common – caring about the world and the people around you. Perhaps you would like to become a politician one day? You never know, maybe a future world leader will start their political journey reading this book!

Eleanor Levenson

Single Transferable Vote

Voters elect more than one person at once and rate the candidates in order of preference by placing a '1' by their first choice, a '2' by their second choice, and so on. Once a candidate has reached the amount of votes needed to win (which is worked out in advance by looking at how many votes have been cast and how many vacancies there are), the remaining votes, and votes of the people who have come last, are redistributed, until all of the vacancies have been filled by reaching the minimum number of votes needed.

VOTING SYSTEMS

There are many different voting systems that
can be used to elect political representatives.
Here are some of them:

First Past The Post
The candidate with the most votes wins,
even if they only have one more vote
than the person who comes second.

Alternative Vote
Voters rate the candidates in order of preference by
placing a '1' by their first choice and a '2' by their second
choice, and so on. If a candidate has over half of the
votes they are the winner. If not, the second choice of
the voters whose first choice came last are added to the
original totals. This continues until one candidate has
more than half of the votes.

Supplementary Vote
Each voter gives a first and second choice candidate. If
no candidate wins over half of the first choice votes, then
everyone is eliminated other than the two candidates with the
most votes, and the second choice votes of people whose first
choice went to the eliminated candidates are added to the
totals of the top two. The winner is the person with the most
votes after these second choices have been included.

POLLING

Political parties often pay polling companies to try to find out what voters think so they can make their policies more appealing. Polling companies also conduct their own surveys to try to predict who will win elections. They do this by asking a sample of people their political views. The company then works out what this would mean if everybody thought in the same way as the people they have asked. For example, if they ask 100 people what they think the most important political issue is at the moment, and two thirds of them say the environment, then they will see this as a sign that two thirds of people in the country probably think this too. In order to make this as accurate as possible they need the 100 people they ask to come from different backgrounds and live in different parts of the country, to make sure they are representative of everybody.

GLOSSARY

Austerity A set of economic policies to help the government spend less, in order to reduce its debts, usually achieved by cutting spending on public services.

Border A line, usually just on a map but it may also follow the line of a geographical feature like a river or mountain range, that marks the separation between States.

Coup d'état This is a French term, often shortened to 'Coup' (pronounced 'Coo'), and means the government has been overthrown, or replaced, using non-democratic means (so not using a legal election).

Diversity When people are different – this can be in terms of their race, religion, gender, sexual orientation, age, physical abilities, political beliefs, wealth, or anything else.

Money A way of paying for goods and services – usually represented by coins and notes – that can be used again by the recipient.

Protest Showing public disapproval or an objection to something that is being imposed on an individual or society.

Reform To make changes to something in the hope of making it better.

Society A group of people who live in the same political, geographical or cultural system.

Speech When a person speaks to an audience, setting out their beliefs in one continuous talk (as opposed to a question and answer session or a conversation).

Tradition A way of doing things that has been passed down from previous generations and is done a certain way because it has always been done that way, rather than for any other reason.

INDEX

FIND OUT MORE

Books

Usborne Politics for Beginners, Alex Frith, Rosie Hore, Louie Stowell (Usborne, 2018)
All About Politics: How Governments Make the World Go Round, DK and Andrew Marr (DK Children, 2016)
No One Is Too Small to Make a Difference, Greta Thunberg (Penguin, 2019)

Websites

youngcitizens.org
A website full of resources for young people, teachers and parents to help us think about democracy and the issues it raises.

https://www.parliament.uk/site-information/glossary/
Explains some of the specific words used in the British Parliamentary System.

https://www.bbc.co.uk/news/politics
Keep on top of news stories about politics so you know what is happening in the world.